IMAGES
of America

THE CRIPPLE CREEK
DISTRICT

CRIPPLE CREEK GOLD DISTRICT.

REFERENCE
Shafts ■ Tunnels ⊙
Scale of Miles

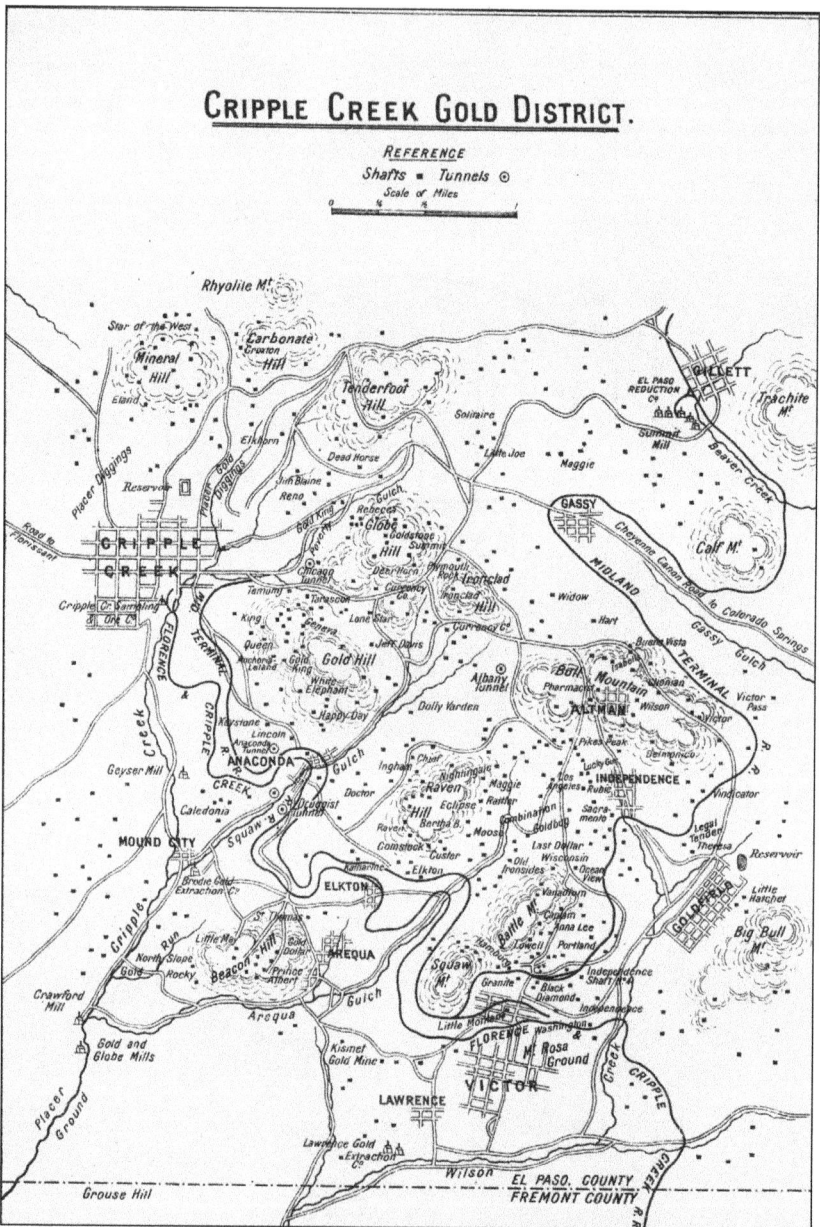

An 1896 map shows most of the towns in the Cripple Creek District, as well as the routes of the Midland Terminal and Florence & Cripple Creek Railroads. This particular map was produced by a British geological survey that came to explore the district. (Courtesy of the Cripple Creek District Museum.)

ON THE COVER: Wildflower excursions and day trips via the Colorado Midland were all the rage among Edwardian-age jet-setters. The trips from Colorado Springs usually included a picnic lunch or a stop at one of the resorts or cafés along the route. Tickets cost $1. The train would travel up Ute Pass to Divide or Lake George and then return, arriving home in time for supper. The train made frequent stops to pick flowers and pause for photographs. (Courtesy of the Cripple Creek District Museum.)

IMAGES
of America

THE CRIPPLE CREEK
DISTRICT

Cripple Creek District Museum

ARCADIA
PUBLISHING

Published by Arcadia Publishing
Charleston, South Carolina

Library of Congress Control Number: 2010939111

For all general information, please contact Arcadia Publishing:
Telephone 843-853-2070
Fax 843-853-0044
E-mail sales@arcadiapublishing.com
For customer service and orders:
Toll-Free 1-888-313-2665

Visit us on the Internet at www.arcadiapublishing.com

*To Blevins Davis, Richard Wayne Johnson, and Dorothy Mackin
for founding the Cripple Creek District Museum and for their
heartfelt dedication to the preservation of our history*

CONTENTS

ACKNOWLEDGMENTS

As a museum, we are very proud of and grateful for all of the people who have worked to preserve our local history over the years. Even today, descendants of our hardy pioneers and fans of our history and the Cripple Creek District Museum continue to maintain close contact with us and support the things we do. However, we never would have come this far and been able to write this book without the following people, who made the museum what it is: Blevins Davis, Richard Johnson, Dorothy Mackin, Wilhelminia and Dr. A.C. "Doc" Denman, Ed Seale, Joan Wilson, Ralph Giddings Jr., Norma Hill, Max Mills, Lucille Mantell, Hazel Bunker, Emma Barr, Vivian Richardson, Gordon Brown, Mary Alice Robinson, Eva Shepard, Leland Feitz, Charles Frizzell, Kenneth "Doc" Yarborough, Lola Fay, Edna Nichols, Dayton Lumis Jr., Erik Swanson, Fern Vetter, Helen Williams, Grace Witcher, Helen Rankin, Lowrena Vetter, Velma McKahan, Mylia and Alfred Orr, Lois Splittstoesser, Laverne and Royce King, Mary Lee Sanders, John Stauss, Jan Pettit, Jean and Norm Sporing, Brian Levine, Vi Whitt, Edith Peiffer, Evelyn Ward, Ken Jahns, Loretta Tremayne, the Shoup family, Ethel Carlton, Troy Wade, Jeff Miller, our board of directors, and countless others.

Participants in this project were William Batok, John Bowman, Corey and Jan Collins, Bonnie and Steve Mackin, Nancy McDonald, Georganna Peiffer, John Sharpe, Marlane B. Smutka, Arthur Tremayne Sr. and his son Richard, Melissa Trenary, and Elizabeth Cassutt Tritz. Each of us worked to select the photographs included here and provide captions to best explain what it was like to live in the World's Greatest Gold Camp. We are all indebted to each other for working as a team and completing the first book to be officially written and published by the Cripple Creek District Museum (CCDM) as a whole.

We are also indebted to the thousands of people from around the world who have donated or loaned to us since 1953 their photographs, personal effects, and artifacts. We thank every one of you for sharing your family histories with us and entrusting us to preserve the district's history for all to enjoy. All images used within this book are from the archives at the Cripple Creek District Museum.

—Jan Collins,
Director of the Cripple Creek District Museum

INTRODUCTION

The history of the region encompassing the Cripple Creek District began 35 million years ago with the eruption of a giant volcano. The explosions from deep in the Earth's core drove vast amounts of mineral ores toward the surface. Hidden within the quartz and granite were rich veins of gold. Time and the elements kept the wealthy deposits buried beneath lush grasslands and forests.

Although gold was discovered in other parts of Colorado as early as the 1850s, the ancient volcano on the western slopes of Pikes Peak went virtually unnoticed until Levi Welty relocated his ranch from the banks of Fountain Creek on the east side of Pikes Peak. The Weltys settled in a lush, rolling valley at the foot of Mount Pisgah in 1871. Mild winters and temperate summers, along with a spring-fed creek running through the property, made the area a perfect place to raise cattle.

A peculiar string of accidents that occurred while building a shed over the spring provided a name for the stream that ran through the ranch. One of the Welty boys was struck by a falling log, injuring his leg. In the commotion, Levi's gun went off, wounding his hand. The gunshot frightened a calf, which jumped into the stream and injured its leg. When the whole episode was over, Levi shook his head and stated, "That is sure some crippled creek."

In the meantime, Robert Miller Womack had come to Colorado from Kentucky with his father in 1861 to prospect in the goldfields west of Denver. The Womacks later went into cattle ranching and eventually took over the Welty Ranch at Cripple Creek. Womack preferred to spend his days riding over the hillsides searching for gold instead of stray cows. When he was not at the ranch, he could be found in the saloons and brothels at Colorado City, now the west side of Colorado Springs.

One day in 1878, Womack was riding on the west side of the ranch in an area that would later be known as Poverty Gulch when he spotted a piece of gold "float." Float is a piece of rock that has broken off from an outcropping and drifted downhill from its original location. The rock was found to be a piece of gold ore worth $200 per ton. Womack was struck with gold fever and spent the next several years tracking the origins of the gold ore. He finally located the vein about two miles up the gulch from where he first saw the float. In the fall of 1886, he staked out a claim and named it the Grand View Lode.

Although the original piece of ore that Womack found was full of gold, no one really believed the story of his discovery. Womack was known to tell tall tales, and the drunker he got, the taller the tales grew. He had a difficult time finding anyone to back him financially. It was several more years before someone believed him and Colorado's last great gold rush began. When it did, the prospectors came in droves.

By 1892, the towns of Fremont and Hayden Placer had been platted on the hillsides to the south and east of Mount Pisgah. The two towns soon merged to become one town, Cripple Creek. Miners, merchants, saloon keepers, and professionals were moving in and setting up shop by the dozens. Nearly 50 mines had started shipping ore. More settlements began popping up as more gold was discovered.

In 1895, the Cripple Creek District boasted a population of 25,000 citizens living in 25 different towns and camps. Two railroads, the Midland Terminal and the Florence & Cripple Creek, were bringing people and supplies into the district and hauling ore from more than 250 mines to mills at Florence and Colorado City. By 1897, two interurban electric railways were servicing the towns of the gold camp. Citizens throughout the district enjoyed the modern conveniences of electricity, telephones, and indoor plumbing. As the 20th century arrived, the population was nearing 50,000, and 475 mines were steadily shipping ore. Total gold production to date exceeded $77 million, or $5.3 billion at today's prices.

Indeed, a former cattle ranch had been transformed into "the World's Greatest Gold Camp" in just eight short years. More than 33 men attained millionaire status seemingly overnight. Winfield Scott Stratton became the first of them with his Independence Mine, which was valued at millions by 1894. In 1898, Stratton sold the mine for a cool $11 million. That year, production from the Cripple Creek gold rush exceeded that of the Sutter's Mill rush in California.

The booming towns on the back of Pikes Peak were not without their share of setbacks. Three massive fires nearly wiped out the two largest cities. Labor wars in 1893 and 1903 threatened to tear the gold camp apart. The latter strike lasted more than a year and turned families, friends, and neighbors against each other. It also marked the beginning of the end of the gold boom.

In time, rising production costs, falling gold prices, and underground water forced many of the mines to close. Bob Womack's death on August 10, 1909, seemed to punctuate the end of the Cripple Creek District's Golden Age. By 1920, less than 50 mines were still shipping ore.

In 1941, the federal government ordered the suspension of all gold mining for the duration of World War II. After the war, many mines remained closed. The last train pulled out of the district in 1949. The year-round population of the district in 1950 had dropped to less than 2,000, as the gold camp became little more than a ghost of its former glory.

With the drop in gold production after the war, citizens of the district made a new discovery: tourism. An annual Donkey Derby Days celebration was created in 1931. Dorothy and Wayne Mackin introduced classic Victorian melodrama in 1948. Curio and souvenir shops, restaurants, and art galleries opened up along Bennett Avenue. The Mollie Kathleen Gold Mine began taking tourists 1,000 feet underground to tour an actual working mine. The Cripple Creek District Museum opened its doors in 1953. Fred and Pat Mentzer purchased Pearl DeVere's famous brothel, the Old Homestead, and opened it as a museum in 1958. The Lowell Thomas Museum opened in the early 1960s. The Cripple Creek & Victor Narrow Gauge Railroad opened in 1967.

In 1974, the United States put an end to the fixed price of gold, and mining was profitable once again. The Cripple Creek and Victor Gold Mining Company was formed, and gold production resumed in 1976. Large-scale open pit mining operations began in 1994, and by 2009, annual gold production had reached 330,000 troy ounces.

The Cripple Creek District went through another transformation in 1991, when Colorado voters approved limited-stakes gambling in the historic mining towns of Black Hawk, Central City, and Cripple Creek. The arrival of gambling marked the beginning of a new boom. Vacant and rundown buildings along Bennett Avenue were given new life, while gaming revenues allowed the city to make much-needed improvements throughout town. Historic preservation funds have provided for extensive restoration of numerous historic commercial and residential buildings.

Museums, family-friendly restaurants, antique stores, curio shops, historic hotels, and bed and breakfasts in both Cripple Creek and Victor, along with Cripple Creek's casinos, make the Cripple Creek District of today a destination for all ages.

—Melissa Trenary
Archivist at the Cripple Creek District Museum

One

From Ranchland to Gold Dust

If ever a piece of land was subject to major upheaval, it was the area comprising the Cripple Creek District. Following the eruption of the great volcano, the district sat virtually dormant for centuries. The scarred and vast landscape was able to reshape, form its mountains, hills, lakes, and creeks, grow foliage and trees, and wait to be discovered by man.

The first humans to actually discover this lovely wonderland were the Native Americans. High open plains, ample water, flint, and mountain cliffs afforded safe, comfortable, and abundant summer quarters. Here the Ute Indians could hunt game, fish, gather wild raspberries and other edible plants, make tools, and post lookouts for enemies with relative ease.

By the time ranchers came to this high country, most of the Native Americans in the area had moved on via Ute Pass, today's Highway 24. White men appreciated not only the wide meadows, but also the rich soil, which offered a short growing season in the high altitude. Ranchers such as the Weltys, the Womacks, and the Carrs found the area conducive to their cattle operations.

When Bob Womack discovered gold, the area next saw a massive influx of gold-seekers, both seasoned prospectors and greenhorns, as they flocked to the district in hopes of seeking their fortunes. The boom not only made history for its time, it also woke up the West and created a household phrase across the entire planet: Cripple Creek!

—Jan Collins
Director of the Cripple Creek District Museum

For some 30 years before gold was discovered in the Cripple Creek District, the region was home to a number of ranches. The high country meadows made excellent grazing pastures for cattle. Here, a group of local cowboys enjoy some time off.

Pioneer rancher Levi Welty later sold his property to the Womacks. When young Robert Womack staked the Grand View Lode, the Cripple Creek District (which was nearly named for him) was established and the gold rush was on. This view shows the Womack homestead several years after the family had moved on and sold the property to real estate developers Horace Bennett and Julius Myers. Today, Bennett Avenue and Myers Avenue remain the main thoroughfares in Cripple Creek.

Denver photographer William Gillen moved to the Cripple Creek District in about 1893 and began photographing several area ranches. Gillen also captured several images of early Cripple Creek and other towns. Pictured above is the Hoyte Ranch in September 1893. Note the great quantity of hay being grown at the ranch.

Gillen also photographed the Tremayne residence on West Four Mile, southwest of Cripple Creek. The Tremaynes have resided in the Cripple Creek District ever since. Arthur Tremayne remains today as the oldest surviving native of Cripple Creek. At the age of 93, he is also a board member at the Cripple Creek District Museum.

George and Emma Carr managed the Pikes Peak Land and Cattle Company, later known as the Houseman Cattle and Land Company, in the late 1880s and early 1890s. The ranch was owned by Bennett and Myers and encompassed most of the valley that is now Cripple Creek. Carr christened the place the Broken Box Ranch and hired Robert Womack for odd jobs. Emma's brother John Edwards is pictured here standing in front of the Carr's home on the ranch.

The Cripple Creek District relied chiefly on stage roads in its early years. The Cheyenne and Beaver Toll Road from Colorado Springs was probably the earliest route, established in 1875. Trips via stagecoach could be long, bumpy, uncomfortable, and even dangerous. As the district grew, supplies and settlers coming from other cities were hauled by wagon trains. In this image, the stage includes luxurious Concord passenger coaches.

The Canon City and Cripple Creek Toll Road was constructed along Shelf Road in 1891 by Canon City businessmen Bill and Ira Lytell. The lower toll keepers' cabin, seen here, was located at the south end of the "shelf" portion of the road. When he would see a stage or freight wagon coming, the toll keeper climbed up the canyon to the road and collected the tolls. The fare ranged from 30¢ for a horse and rider to $1.75 for a six-horse stage and was collected at both ends.

The Hundley Stage Line traveled south between the railroad stop of Divide and the Cripple Creek District. The Halfway House was located about seven miles south of Divide. Stages and freighters would stop here to change horses and pay the toll. When the Midland Terminal Railroad was built as a spur from the Colorado Midland Railroad at Divide, the small settlement of Midland was established on this site.

Upon achieving his dream as the discoverer of gold at Cripple Creek, Robert Womack led the life of a celebrity. He was, unfortunately, prone to selling his claims at ridiculously low prices and spending his money freely, likely under the assumption that he would always find more. Womack eventually ended up at his sister Lida's quaint boardinghouse in Colorado Springs, where he died virtually penniless in 1909.

Some early miners to the Cripple Creek District tried their hands at placer mining. This method of mining involved scooping dirt and gravel into a shaker or sluice box and running water across it. The gold would separate from the gravel and sink to the bottom. Placer mining was short-lived. Miners soon discovered that due to the unique mineralization caused by the eruption of the ancient volcano, gathering Cripple Creek gold required digging and blasting.

Early mines of the Cripple Creek District were hastily constructed of area timber. The Blue Bell Mine, pictured above, was among the earliest claims staked in 1892, and ranchman George Carr was an investor.

Assayers gained popularity in the Cripple Creek District because they could quickly assess how much gold a ton of rock was likely to yield. The assayer usually charged a fee or a percentage of the gold for performing the process. Chemicals were applied to a small amount of rock, melting it and leaving the gold behind. This assayer is identified as both William Hoyt and H. Dana. Hoyt had previously worked in Alma, Colorado, before coming to Cripple Creek. Dana worked for the Abe Lincoln Mine in the Cripple Creek District.

As the Cripple Creek gold rush came into full swing, people came in droves to make their riches. Single miners, couples, and families packed their worldly possessions to the Cripple Creek District in hopes of finding gold. Many, such as this unidentified couple, initially lived in tents until they could afford something better.

Sawmills eventually began supplying cut lumber for construction of shaft houses at the mines, business buildings, and homes. These early cabins, photographed by William Gillen on March 15, 1894, depict Frank Banta's tiny mining camp near Cripple Creek. The foursquare, framed windows were likely purchased from a catalog or manufacturer and hauled to the district. The man on the far right with the dog is thought to be Frank Banta.

Within a short time, homesteads were dotting the landscape all over the Cripple Creek District. Pioneer prospectors tended to build their homes as close to their mining claims as possible; thus, a person traipsing through the forest could come upon someone's house at any time. Most families were forced to share small quarters until they could afford to build a larger home.

Before long, homes in the district towns of Cripple Creek, Victor, Goldfield, and others were beginning to resemble Victorian homes in larger cities. Houses began taking on such fancy adornments as milled lumber siding, bay windows, gables, and dormers. Note the child peering from behind the curtain of this Cripple Creek home.

Fremont was the first town established in the Cripple Creek District, until a competing land developer established another community nearby and called it Hayden Placer. Unlike Fremont, Hayden Placer outlawed saloons and gambling houses, which may explain why the population of the latter town was considerably smaller. This image, taken in or around July 1892, was captured from Tenderfoot Hill looking into the volcanic valley.

This is the earliest known photograph of Fremont up close. The image was taken showing the town to the east. Bennett Avenue, the main drag, figures prominently in the picture. Note the buildings are all constructed of wood and canvas. A month later, the communities of Fremont and Hayden Placer had been melded into one town.

Donkeys have been an integral part of mining throughout the ages. These sure-footed little creatures were a very reliable form of transportation and able to climb narrow, steep slopes that horses and mules could not. Their ability to carry nearly half their weight made them an invaluable asset in the mining camps. Donkeys were also used underground in the mines. Their compact size and stamina allowed them to move easily through the tunnels.

Brothers Vernon and Homer Peiffer first settled in the Cripple Creek District in the early 1890s. Their first business venture was transporting supplies, mainly Niff Beer, from Canon City up the Shelf Toll Road to the district. Later the Peiffers opened a bottling works and even produced ice cream. The men of the family also became very prominent in business and civic affairs.

Winfield Scott Stratton was the first millionaire in the district. A friend of Bob Womack, Stratton was divorced and making a meager living as a carpenter when he first came to Cripple Creek. On July 4, 1891, he staked the Independence Mine, which brought him an amazing amount of wealth. Even so, Stratton himself once said, "Too much money is not good for any man. I have too much, and it is not good for me." The unhappy millionaire became an alcoholic recluse. This is the last known portrait of Stratton, who died on September 14, 1902, at the young age of 54.

Winfield Scott Stratton's Independence Mine was one of the earliest and wealthiest mines in the Cripple Creek District. In time, the Independence became the third-largest producer in the district, with a gross production of $28 million by 1951. Likewise, Stratton's American Eagles Mine, pictured above, was comprised of 32 acres and seven claims.

Two

THE BUILDING
OF THE BOOMTOWNS

On an evening in 1905, City Marshal John Sharpe stepped out of Cripple Creek City Hall and looked east on Bennett Avenue. He marveled at the changes that had occurred since he came here in 1891. The gold strike was just starting. Sharpe had rented a bed at the only hotel in town, a two-story log structure that later burned in the fires of 1896. During those early years, he had been one of hundreds, then thousands, that rushed to the World's Greatest Gold Camp.

Now there were nearly 50,000 souls inhabiting a number of communities. From their humble beginnings as ranches, the discovery of gold had transformed these places into one of the largest gold districts to ever exist. Tranquil pastures were replaced by the roar of dynamite and clamor of trains, hammers, and saws until the district became a bustling metropolis. More than 500 mines produced millions of dollars in gold annually.

Schools, churches, stores, newspapers, saloons, hotels, restaurants, and theaters snuggled among hundreds of wood and brick houses that surrounded downtowns full of every type of enterprise, both legal and semi-legal. Before and after the fires that wiped out both Cripple Creek and Victor, all attempts were made to construct modern cities built for modern times. Cripple Creek in particular became so affluent that it outranked Denver for a time and nearly became the new capital of Colorado.

Marshal Sharpe had watched the district evolve. He had been involved with it all. He had run mines, built houses, and owned a couple of businesses. At the turn of the century, he played an integral part in shutting down gambling as the cities of the district tried to keep up with the rest of the country.

And still, pioneers continued to flock to the district, stake their claims, make their money, and live their lives in a boom camp.

—John Sharpe (grandson of Marshal John Sharpe)
Board member of the Cripple Creek District Museum
and Marlane B. Smutka
Docent of the Cripple Creek District Museum

Mound City was one of the district's earliest mining camps, settled in 1891 at the bottom of Squaw Gulch. At the time this photograph was taken in 1893, roughly 400 people called Mound City home. There was a general store, a one-room schoolhouse, two mills, and four hotels. Eventually, Mound City was absorbed by the larger town of Anaconda to the east.

In 1892, M.S. Raynolds of Denver purchased a large chunk of the Victor C. Adams homestead and platted the town of Lawrence. When the nearby town of Victor was platted out of the rest of Adams's homestead in 1893, the communities grew together. Lawrence's population never exceeded 300 residents, most of them miners.

In February 1892, real estate tycoons Horace Bennett and Julius Myers platted a town at Arequa. Lots were sold for a total profit of $320,000. This image, taken in 1892, is the only known photograph of Arequa. In actuality, the town had a post office for only two months, and the town never boasted more than 100 residents.

Houses and other structures are just beginning to spring up in this early image of Cripple Creek. On the middle right, the business buildings of downtown can be seen. In the foreground, square cabins with rounded roofs form neighborhoods. These early homes may have actually been the prefabricated houses of yesteryear. The materials were ordered by catalog, hauled by wagon, and assembled on site.

BARRY. BAND. COMING IN TO CRIPPLE CREEK NOV 24TH 32.

Horace Barry realized at least some of his dreams when his namesake town sported its own marching band. The Barry Band made its debut at parades in towns throughout the Cripple Creek District. The town of Barry also had a social club, some saloons, and a few stores, as well as a small red-light district.

Houses and other structures are just beginning to spring up in this early image of Cripple Creek. On the middle right, the business buildings of downtown can be seen. In the foreground, square cabins with rounded roofs are forming neighborhoods. These early homes may have actually been the prefabricated houses of yesteryear. The materials were ordered by catalog, hauled by wagon, and assembled on-site.

During 1893, Cripple Creek saw an even more dramatic increase in business houses and population. Pictured here is the S.F. Faulkner Livery and Feed Stable, captured by photographer William Gillen. The Faulkners were a large family and remained in the livery business at Cripple Creek for more than two decades.

The town of Altman is visible perched on the edge of Bull Hill above Victor. The town was founded in September 1893 and named for sawmill operator Sam Altman, who also purchased mines in the area. At an altitude of 10,700 feet, Altman once held the record as the highest incorporated city in the United States.

Pictured above is Altman's main street in 1893. A number of businesses and residents, including attorneys, dry goods stores, saloons, restaurants, and hotels, managed to survive Altman's high altitude. There was even a telephone available at Morrison and McMillan's store. Altman served as a stronghold for union miners during the labor wars of 1893–1894.

A group of pioneers gather on the railroad tracks overlooking the town of Anaconda around 1900. Anaconda was located halfway between Cripple Creek and Victor, making it a popular stopover between the towns and attractive to miners and their families. The town eventually absorbed the small communities around it, including Barry, Mound City, Jackpot, and Glory Hole. Anaconda incorporated in 1894.

By 1897, people were using any means available to get to the Cripple Creek District to find their fortunes. Modes of transportation evolved as the population grew. In this image of Anaconda, taken by photographer William Henry Jackson, trains, stagecoaches, horses, and rough-hewn roads represent common methods of travel.

The tiny hamlet of Midway was so named for its location between Cripple Creek and the town of Independence. Midway's best-known resident in later years was "French Blanche" LeCroix, a former Cripple Creek prostitute who suffered acid burns at the hands of a jealous wife. Blanche is wearing the plaid apron, flanked on either side by Blanche Koech, Maude Calhoun, Bill Lehr, and two unidentified women. Blanche's Midway home, the only surviving building from the town, is now located at the Cripple Creek District Museum. (Special thanks to Dianne Hartshorn of BlachesPlace.com.)

In the early years of Cripple Creek, the eastern portion of Myers Avenue was a respectable area of town. Attorney's offices, furniture stores, millinery shops, hardware stores, blacksmith shops, and feed stores lined the street. In 1894, the city fathers ordered all prostitution be moved off Bennett Avenue down to Myers Avenue, transforming the once-decent business district into one of Colorado's most infamous red-light districts.

Brothers Leslie and Albert Carlton made their mark on Cripple Creek early on with the opening of their Colorado Trading & Transfer Company on the corner of Fifth Street and Bennett Avenue. Built in 1894 as a hay and feed store, the building was later transformed into a top railroad freight company under the Carltons. Here, teamsters gather outside the main building (now a part of the Cripple Creek District Museum) to load and unload freight.

Over time, the Colorado Trading & Transfer Company employed hundreds of freighters and teamsters. These hardy men drove wagons, loaded and unloaded tons of supplies and ore on the trains, hauled freight to the outlying towns in the Cripple Creek District, and made hundreds of trips between Cripple Creek and the mines of the district each day.

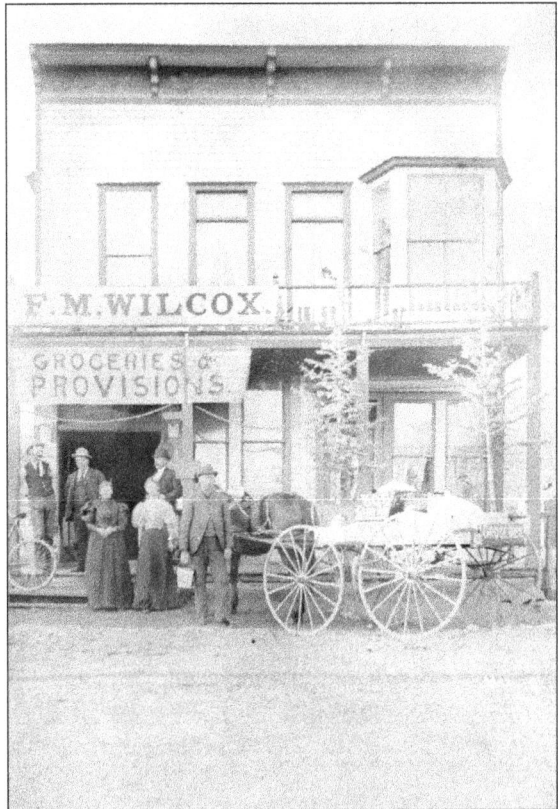

Fortice M. Wilcox and his son Bert owned and operated one of Cripple Creek's first grocery stores at 505 Carr Avenue. The family resided directly above the store, a typical living situation for most merchants and business owners throughout the district. The building pictured here likely burned in Cripple Creek's fires of 1896.

31

The town of Independence was originally platted as Hull City in 1894. When the city of Goldfield was platted in close proximity a short time later, both towns quickly grew together. While Goldfield served as a suburb of Victor, Independence functioned as another workingman's town.

Rufus Porter, also known as "the Hardrock Poet," identified this lady on horseback as "the Queen of Independence." Porter began mining in the Cripple Creek District in 1917 and made a second career writing about the area. Of the Queen of Independence, he wrote, "She recalls seeing two gamblers relaxing one morning after a hard night's work. They each had a stack of gold pieces over a foot high piled on the sidewalk, and they were spitting at a crack in the walk—for $20 a spit."

The community of Love was named for a rancher's spread located in Beaver Park at the very edge of the Cripple Creek District. First a stage road and later the Colorado Springs & Cripple Creek District Railroad serviced the tiny hamlet. A post office, school, and store served the community from 1894 to 1902.

Students pose in front of the Love School. In no order, those identified in the photograph are Mattie Mitchell, Lew Beasley, Celon Hoy, Lydia Beasley, Stella Shacklett, Hattie Mitchell, Bert Beasley, John Shepard, Bessie Beasley, and Art Taylor. Harry Spur, Mollie, Lela Mitchell, Pete Renico, Mabel Ferguson, William Renico, George Smith, Warren Gregory, Ceylon Stumpff, Frankie Ferguson, Lizzie, Cassie Renico, Laura Renico, and George Shaw. Today, the Franklin Ferguson Library in Cripple Creek is named for Frankie Ferguson, who was later a mayor of Cripple Creek.

REAR GUARD AT MIDLAND.

Early plat maps of Midland, located nearly halfway between Cripple Creek and Divide, show plans for a grand hotel and depot. In this image, taken in 1893, the hotel and depot appear to be in one building. When the Midland Terminal Railroad came through, the former stage stop became nothing more than a water stop for the trains.

The city of Victor, founded in 1893 as a workingman's mining town, grew to be the second-largest city in the Cripple Creek District. Like Cripple Creek, Victor was platted quickly on a series of hillsides. The terrain made construction of a level building difficult. Photographer A.P. Martin, whose studio is shown here in 1894, made the best of his location by building on stilts.

The Florence & Cripple Creek Railroad, winding its way through the steep curves of Phantom Canyon from Florence, made history as the first train to reach Cripple Creek. The train managed to reach an area half a mile outside of Cripple Creek on June 30, 1894. The next day, a photographer captured hundreds of residents milling around the locomotive. Unfortunately, the train suffered a derailment on July 2 as it returned to Victor, killing one person and injuring 21 others.

With more than 500 active mines in the Cripple Creek District, the hillsides became literal honeycombs. Cave-ins and sinkholes were commonplace. This unfortunate accident along the High Line Interurban Electric Rail was caused when a stope (tunnel) in the Logan Mine on Bull Hill collapsed.

Gillett was platted in July 1894. The town was named for W.K. Gillett of the Midland Terminal Railroad, which was built through the town on its way to the Cripple Creek District. Famous Cripple Creek madam Pearl DeVere got her start here, as did hundreds of miners, attorneys, and shopkeepers. Churches, schools, hotels, and even a racetrack rounded out the amenities. In 1895, Gillett became famous for staging the only "legal" bullfight in the United States.

The depot for the Midland Terminal Railroad, the second railroad to reach the Cripple Creek District, opened in December 1895. The building was (and still is) the fanciest railroad depot in the area. Upwards of 94 trains rolled through daily, making the Midland Terminal the largest and most productive railroad in the district. Today, the depot is preserved as part of the Cripple Creek District Museum.

Above is a view of East Myers Avenue, looking west from the Colorado Midland Terminal railroad tracks, around 1898. As the heart of Cripple Creek's red-light district for more than 30 years, Myers Avenue was well known for its houses of prostitution, saloons, and gambling houses. In 1898, respectable citizens of Myers successfully appealed to the city council to change the name to Masonic Avenue west of Third Street.

Carlton's Colorado Trading & Transfer Company of Cripple Creek was able to expand within just a few years. A branch office opened in Victor in about 1895 and was soon brimming with business. Albert Carlton was a millionaire by the age of 33 and even owned his own bank in Cripple Creek.

The Eagle Sampler, pictured here in 1895, was located above Goldfield. The mine was large enough to support a small community known as Eagle Junction. Later, the Colorado Springs & Cripple Creek District Railroad extended a spur to the Eagle Sampler. The clean, large mine buildings in this image are representative of hundreds of others that dotted the landscape throughout the district.

Victor, dubbed "the City of Mines," was growing by October 1894. This early image shows the fledgling city while it was still under construction. The picture was taken looking south toward Grouse Mountain.

This image gives an example of home life in Cripple Creek during the late 1800s. A small log cabin like this would seem crude and primitive by Eastern standards, but with a woman's touch, early homes became quite comfortable over time. Most were well chinked on the outside and insulated inside with burlap or newspapers. A wood- or coal-burning stove could keep the cabin warm and cozy during the worst Colorado winter nights.

The Brodie Mill at Mound City was the first gold mill in the Cripple Creek District. By 1897, the Brodie had doubled its capacity to process ore, going through 175 to 200 tons per day. The mill closed in 1899, but it reopened in 1900 as the Centennial Gold Extraction Company. The new mill could turn out 1,800 tons of ore per month.

Established in 1895 as a family-oriented community, Goldfield was the third-largest city in the Cripple Creek District. This image, taken in 1897, shows the extent of the largely residential township. Much calmer and quieter than its neighboring communities, Goldfield had more churches and civic meeting places than dance halls and saloons. In its infancy, the town also had a "pest house" where people were quarantined during epidemics.

Some of the unfortunate but necessary services in an often violent living and working environment were provided by the St. Nicholas Hospital in Cripple Creek. A much smaller hospital was initially established in a two-story home in 1894. For years, the Catholic Sisters of Mercy appealed to the citizens of the district for money to build a bigger, better hospital to meet the growing needs of area residents. The new St. Nicholas, shown here, was completed in 1898.

Above are images of Car No. 3, the *Clement*, on the electric line. The *Clement* suffered a wreck in 1898. On the way down Gold Hill, the conductor saw Car No. 2, the *Grace*, careening out of control toward him. The conductor and the motorman were pulling on the brake in a vain attempt to slow the *Grace* down, and several passengers had jumped from the car. The conductor of the *Clement* quickly ordered his passengers off. He started down the hill in front of the *Grace*, hoping to gain enough momentum to stop it when the two collided. When they did, the *Grace* did

stop, but the *Clement*'s brakes gave way and the car began hurtling down toward Cripple Creek as the conductor frantically rang a warning bell. A six-horse wagon barely cleared the tracks as the car barreled toward Fifth Street. The motorman and conductor both jumped out at Poverty Gulch. The *Clement* stayed on course as it careened down Myers but finally jumped the tracks at Second Street, landing on its side and sliding another block before stopping. There were several injuries, but nobody was killed.

In 1899, the Woods brothers began construction of Skaguay Reservoir, across Beaver Creek, for a power plant. A pipeline, made of redwood planks wrapped with metal bands, ran some five miles to the plant. The dam was the largest of its kind in the world and provided the entire Cripple Creek District with power. A massive flood in 1965 forced moss and rock into Skaguay, filling two miles of pipeline with sediment and closing the power plant.

The Economic Gold Extraction Company rises above homes in Eclipse. Built by Victor founders Harry and Frank Woods, the mill was one of the first to use a chlorination process to refine gold in the district. The small town of Eclipse was established for miners who worked at the mill. Eclipse was eventually absorbed by the nearby town of Elkton.

When the Cripple Creek District was first formed, it did so under the auspices of El Paso County. For years, mine owners and residents of the district rallied to form their own county. Naturally, the move received resistance from El Paso County, which benefited from the district's growing wealth. The district ultimately succeeded in forming Teller County in March 1899. Here, a crowd gathers at the grand opening celebration of the Teller County Courthouse in 1901.

The community of Cameron had its beginnings as a place name known as Grassy or sometimes Gassy. The Woods Investment Company of Victor purchased the land in 1899 and established the town. A small, rural population merited mention in the 1900 district directory. Cameron is shown here in its formative years, but the town never amounted to much as a residential destination.

A creation by the Woods brothers, Pinnacle Park was built near Cameron in 1900 as an amusement park for residents of the Cripple Creek District. The railroad brought folks to the park on the weekends. Amusements included a dance pavilion, restaurant, and carnival games. There was also a zoo, which exhibited native wildlife that included deer, bears, and even mountain lions.

The southeast corner of Fourth Street and Victor Avenue in Victor was a very busy place. The Palace Pharmacy was prominent in both Victor and Cripple Creek and served residents for a number of years. Dr. J. Wallace Collins worked as a physician and surgeon in Victor as late as 1900.

Following a catastrophic fire in Victor in August 1899, the Victor Bank opened on Christmas Eve. The new, four-story, modern building was completed in just four months. The structure is still occupied partly as office space and partly as the grand Victor Hotel.

Above is a panoramic view of Victor around 1900. The city was home to more than 5,000 people. Dubbed the "City of Mines," Victor was a true workingman's town and home to more miners than Cripple Creek. Today, Victor remains one of the best-preserved and charming towns in Colorado.

Strattonville, also known as Winfield, was founded by millionaire Winfield Scott Stratton. Determined that miners should live and work in safe and comfortable conditions, Stratton established his own company town during the late 1890s. There were no saloons or gambling houses at Strattonville, which may explain why the peak population in 1900 was only 100 people. This image shows Strattonville in the 1970s, long after it was abandoned. Shortly after this photograph was taken, mining operations razed the town.

48

Day shift workers pause outside the Republic Mine. Most miners in the Cripple Creek District worked under dangerous conditions. A cave-in, poisonous gas, or misfired explosion could cause serious injury or death. The average pay was $3 per day for a 12-hour shift. Hazardous working conditions and low pay led to two strikes: one in 1893 and another in 1903.

For many years, outlying towns of the Cripple Creek District were linked by two electric trolley lines under the Golden Circle Electric Railway. The lines were more commonly known as the High Line and the Low Line. The fare was a nickel, affording quick and easy access to nearly all of the towns and camps within the district. The High Line was the highest interurban system in the country, peaking at an elevation of 10,487 feet.

Constructed in 1901, the Colorado Springs & Cripple Creek District Railroad provided the most direct route to the district from Colorado Springs. The Short Line, as it was called, was constructed in response to ever-rising freight charges imposed by the Midland Terminal Railroad. The route was very scenic and inspired future president Theodore Roosevelt, after taking a trip on the line in 1901, to comment, "This is the ride that bankrupts the English language!"

To alleviate the crowded hospitals in the district, Teller County Hospital was completed in 1902 at a cost of a little under $20,000. The hospital was in operation until August 1961. In 1967, Wayne and Dorothy Mackin bought it and transformed the former hospital into a grand hotel. Today, the Cripple Creek Hospitality House and RV Park hosts hotel guests, campers, and numerous functions during the summer months.

The Teller County Jail was constructed in Cripple Creek in 1902. The new "gray bar hotel" sported 14 cells in the main cell block, a women's holding area with three cells, and an infirmary. The jail was deemed "inhumane" in 1992 and closed down. Today, it functions as a museum.

Although gold production had started to decline by 1911, Cripple Creek was still a booming metropolis. Thousands called the fine city home. Every modern amenity was available in the city, including one of the first stores of the May Department Stores Company. In this image, the tallest mountain visible is Mount Pisgah, and the Collegiate Peaks can be seen in the background.

The seventh-largest producing mine in the Cripple Creek District was the Elkton, shown here in 1919. The town of Elkton was founded in April 1895 by William Shemwell, who owned the mine. The town soon grew to absorb the nearby communities of Arequa, Eclipse, and Beacon Hill. Elkton, as well as the mountain on which it sat, was demolished by mining operations in 1994.

Three

THE GREAT FIRES

Fire! The greatest fear and threat to the prosperity of any boomtown was fire. Whether it was Virginia City, Nevada, or Helena, Montana, few towns escaped the ravages of this most deadly disaster. The towns of the Cripple Creek District were no exception and suffered many of these catastrophes.

Cripple Creek itself suffered several devastating conflagrations. In addition to an 1892 fire, which destroyed seven buildings on Bennett Avenue, other small-scale burns also occurred: in 1940, the Cripple Creek Mortuary burned down, taking the life of police chief Morris Dolan, and the Grubstake Hotel (also known as the Welty Block) was consumed by fire in 1976.

None of these events, however, compare to the fires of 1896. On April 25, a fire that started in a dance hall within the city's infamous red-light district on Myers Avenue leveled nearly a quarter of the town. Four days later, on the 29th, another conflagration occurred, this one starting in the kitchen of the Portland Hotel and annihilating nearly all that was left of the town. More than 5,000 were left homeless out of a total population of approximately 10,000. The timely assistance of Winfield Scott Stratton, the acknowledged "King of Cripple Creek," was largely responsible for preventing this atrocity from setting the city back for months, rather than just days. Stratton's relief trains were loaded and rolling toward Cripple Creek even before the fire was out.

On August 29, 1899, fire wiped out approximately three-quarters of the district's second-largest city, Victor. Like Cripple Creek, Victor was rebuilt quickly and effectively; what had been ramshackle wood buildings thrown together out of any available materials became thoroughly modern structures made of brick and stone.

The town of Anaconda was less fortunate. With the production of gold already on the decline across the district, the fire of 1904 destroyed a city already in recession, and little or no effort was made to rebuild it. Instead, residents simply moved on, either to the other remaining townships or out of the area entirely.

—William Batok
Archivist at the Cripple Creek District Museum

Prior to the fires of 1896, Cripple Creek was well on its way to becoming a first-class modern town. Pictured here is Bennett Avenue, looking east at what is known as "the Terrace." The building with the two rounded tops on the left is Becker & Nolon's Saloon, located at Bennett Avenue an Third Street. It was said that Becker and Nolon suffered the biggest losses in town in the wake of the fires.

On April 25, 1896, a dance hall girl named Jennie LaRue tousled with her paramour in her room at the Central Dance Hall on Myers Avenue. The two kicked over a gasoline stove, which quickly spread throughout the ramshackle wood building. Within a very short time, Cripple Creek's notorious red-light district was on fire. Here, observers watch as the fire is just beginning.

Smoke billows onto Bennett Avenue as the fire sweeps out of control. This image, looking east, captures the confusion and mayhem of the downtown district. Goods were piled in the street in an attempt to keep them out of the path of the flames. Several carts are visible as they are loaded with items in anticipation of the coming flames.

The April 25, 1986, fire consumed roughly 30 acres. Becker & Nolon's Saloon, the Cripple Creek Mining Exchange, the First National Bank, and the post office all burned, as well as other businesses and approximately 30 homes. This view was taken from the Midland Terminal Railroad trestle above Myers Avenue.

The second of Cripple Creek's two great fires began on Wednesday, April 29, 1896, at the Portland Hotel near the corner of Warren Avenue and Second Street. A kitchen maid accidentally knocked over a pot of grease on the stove, immediately setting the building ablaze. Others, however, speculated that the fire had been started on purpose in growing efforts among unscrupulous citizens to cash in on insurance money.

The first fire had depleted Cripple Creek's water supply in the large reservoir above town. During the second fire, firefighters resorted to dynamiting several buildings in the commercial district to prevent the flames from spreading. Here, black billows of smoke roll out of the El Paso Livery Stable as it is blown to smithereens. The photographer was lucky enough to capture the image at the exact moment of the explosion.

Moments after the El Paso Livery Stable explosion, the same photographer took another photograph showing even more smoke filling the sky. Those whose homes were in the way of the flames were instructed to get to the reservoir as quickly as possible. The city was in total mayhem for several hours. The injured were taken to St. Nicholas Hospital for treatment. Firemen surrounded the hospital to stave off the flames, thereby saving the hospital from burning.

This is a view of Cripple Creek shortly after the great fires. The photograph was taken from the northwest part of town, in the area of West Golden Avenue and North First Street. In just four days, nearly two-thirds of the town had been laid to waste and more than 5,000 citizens had lost their businesses and homes.

Above is another angle of the fire's destruction, taken from the back lot of the Colorado Trading & Transfer Company building and looking west on Myers Avenue. Per Leslie and Albert Carlton's decree, the Trading & Transfer was saved from burning even as buildings around it were dynamited. The Trading & Transfer building survives as the only wooden commercial structure in Cripple Creek today and is part of the Cripple Creek District Museum.

The reconstruction of Cripple Creek was an amazing time. Within just weeks, citizens cleaned up the rubbish-piled streets and began rebuilding modern, safe, brick buildings. Most businesses had reopened within just a few days, and new buildings towered throughout the business district within a matter of months. Even today, a city ordinance decrees that all commercial buildings must be built of brick.

Cripple Creek may have thought it had rid itself of its detested red-light district following the fires, but authorities were wrong. Many of Cripple Creek's madams were insured, enabling them to build bigger and better houses of prostitution. This image reflects massive construction going on along Myers Avenue, including that of the infamous Old Homestead Parlor House.

Despite the growing wealth of the Cripple Creek District, the fires of 1896 devastated city coffers. Checks written by the city were passed around by second and third parties until they could clear the bank. It was two years before the city was able to rebuild its city hall, which premiered in 1898, complete with offices, the Central Fire Station, and even quarters upstairs for the firemen.

The new and improved Central Fire Station was large and roomy. Two fire horses, Buck and Dutch, are shown here demonstrating the upgraded cable-and-pulley system that set the harness. The horses were stabled inside the firehouse. They were trained to step from their stalls to their position in front of the fire wagon when the alarmed sounded. The harness was then lowered by cables from the ceiling onto their backs. The whole process, from the sounding of the alarm until the horses and wagon were out the door, took less than five minutes.

The Westside Fire Station, better known as Fire Station No. 3, was built on West Masonic Avenue in 1900. The station was initially home to Hose Company No. 2 from 1901 until about 1913. Some of the men in the photograph are identified as Harry "Butch" De Cordova, Judge E.W. Lewis, Frank Ellis, Jim McCormack, Scott Lemon, Jack Murphy, and Lon Bates.

Another of the Cripple Creek Fire Department's historic horse teams was Mandy and Bess, shown here at Fire Station No. 3. The horses were taken for daily walks while their stalls were cleaned. Firemen at the station kept daily logbooks to record weather conditions, what time they took their dinner breaks, what work was performed during their shift, and how many fire calls were made.

The Warren Fire Station was located at the corner of Warren Avenue and First Street on the south side of town. Altogether there were four fire stations in Cripple Creek. All were geographically situated to protect the town in its entirety. From 1894 to about 1901, the Warren Station was home to Hose Company No. 2. The station was just big enough to house a wagon and two horses.

Like Cripple Creek, Victor also suffered a major fire at the hands of a "lady of easy virtue." On August 21, 1899, a fire broke out at a dance hall in Paradise Alley at Third Street and Portland Avenue. Note that the two painters working at the Gold Coin Club (large, white building at the lower right) are apparently not yet aware of the coming inferno. The Gold Coin and its namesake mine later succumbed to the flames.

Victor's fire quickly burned out of control, emitting plumes of smoke into the air. Goods from the burning business district were quickly loaded onto Florence & Cripple Creek Railroad boxcars and moved outside of town. Even the Cripple Creek Fire Department came to help. Still, the losses were great.

Residents poke around in the ashes in the aftermath of the Victor fire. The entire business district, two railroad stations, and 300 other buildings were burned. The damages amounted to more than $2 million. Four men died from smoke inhalation, and countless others were injured. Within a few days, however, Victor's most important businesses had reopened, and the city began recovering from the fire.

This undated image shows the town of Altman on fire. Several other towns, mines, and structures in the Cripple Creek District suffered fires, both small and large. Among them was Anaconda, which burned in 1904 and was only partially rebuilt.

The luxurious living quarters at the Central Fire Station in Cripple Creek are shown here around 1905. Firemen were treated with utmost respect by most citizens. Their jobs not only included fighting fires but also seeing to the safety of local citizens. Firemen were friends with everyone, from the esteemed citizens of the town down to the red-light ladies of Myers Avenue.

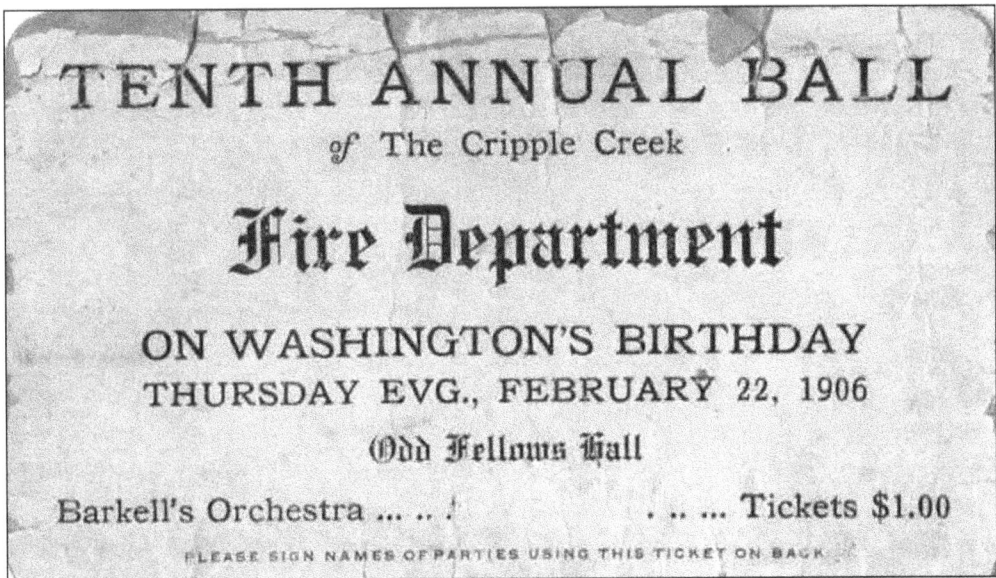

TENTH ANNUAL BALL

of The Cripple Creek

Fire Department

ON WASHINGTON'S BIRTHDAY
THURSDAY EVG., FEBRUARY 22, 1906

Odd Fellows Hall

Barkell's Orchestra ... . Tickets $1.00

PLEASE SIGN NAMES OF PARTIES USING THIS TICKET ON BACK

For more than a century, the Cripple Creek Fire Department hosted an annual firemen's ball as a fundraiser. The soiree was usually held at one of the local theaters or lodges and included dancing to a live band. Few missed out on the chance to buy tickets. Later celebrations included competitions such as tug-of-war or racing a hose cart up and down Bennett Avenue. Firemen often traveled to other cities around the state to engage in such competitions.

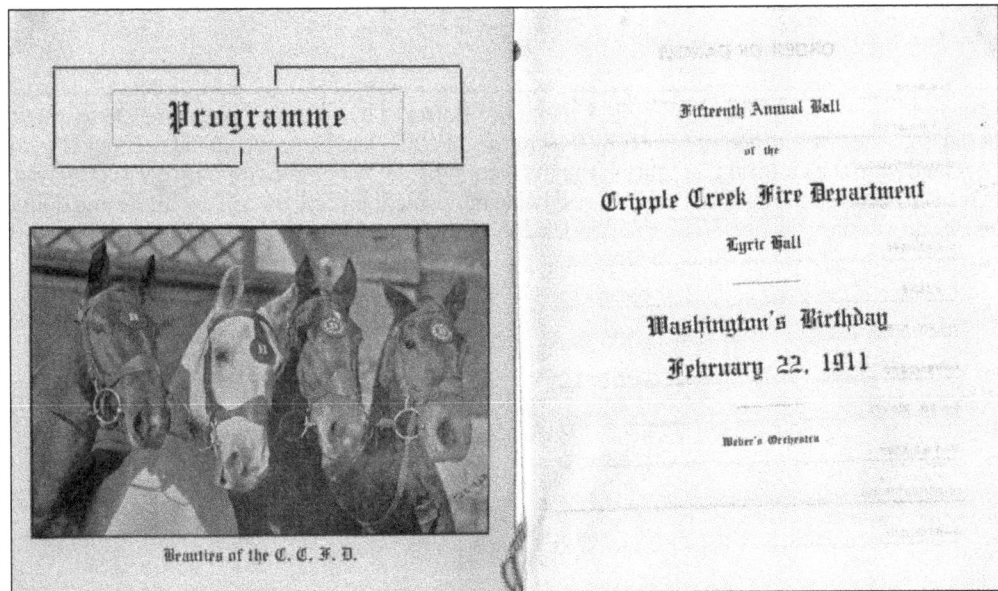

Programme

Fifteenth Annual Ball

of the

Cripple Creek Fire Department

Lyric Hall

Washington's Birthday
February 22, 1911

Weber's Orchestra

Beauties of the C. C. F. D.

The program for the 1911 firemen's ball included a salute to Cripple Creek's fire horses, captioned here as "Beauties of the C.C.F.D." From left to right are Bess, Mandy, Doc, and Dan. Due to their highly trained skills, fire horses tended to be respected as much as their human counterparts. The fire horses received daily grooming, exercise, and treats, and they were loved by everyone.

Doc and Dan were the last of Cripple Creek's fire horses. The Cripple Creek Fire Department purchased a new White Motor Company fire engine in 1912. Doc, Dan, and an old fire wagon were relocated from the Central Fire Station to Fire Station No. 3. When the fire wagon was taken out of service a few years later, Doc and Dan still held employment pulling the city sprinkler and doing other odd jobs for the city. Here, the famous duo was captured by a photographer in 1905.

In this photograph, members of the Cripple Creek Fire Department show off one of the new fire trucks in 1912. The old fire wagons eventually passed into private hands and were converted to farm or freight wagons. One of them, a 1909 Seagrave, is preserved today at the Cripple Creek District Museum.

Roy Bourquin, right, was Cripple Creek's resident pyromaniac. As a boy, he took a hammer to a stick of dynamite and blew off both his arms. Bourquin was labeled incorrigible, and his parents abandoned him at the Sisters of Mercy Hospital, where he became a ward of the state. He was transferred to the Teller County Hospital around 1918. Shortly afterwards, the staff caught him in the basement, stacking dynamite on the furnace in an attempt to blow up the boilers. Bourquin was eventually transferred to the Colorado State Mental Hospital. In 1930, he was at the Colorado State Penitentiary in Canon City, and what became of him is unknown.

Cripple Creek's mortuary on Bennett Avenue burned in 1940, resulting in a total loss. In this image, young Bud Peiffer (right) and his friend Troy Wade Jr. are witnesses to the aftermath of the fire. Peiffer was told by his mother that he could not go downtown to watch the fire, but he snuck out anyway and was consequently caught in the cameraman's lens. Peiffer said he was "in a heap of trouble" when his mother saw the photograph in the newspaper the following morning.

Four

LIFE IN THE DISTRICT

Georganna Peiffer's parents, Ulmer and Isabell McCleerey, came to Victor in 1930. Ulmer owned Mac's Barber Shop in Cripple Creek, but the family frequently moved between there and Victor.

Growing up in the district, Georganna saw many remnants of what life was once like for pioneer families. Old-fashioned home remedies, recipes, and ways of life were instilled in her as a young child. "My earliest memories are of being in second grade at the Washington School in Victor," she said. "The next year we moved into the 'Big School [the Victor High School],' as they had combined grades one through 12."

Indeed, the number of abandoned schools throughout the district signified how large the student population had once been. Once-prominent homes illustrated wealthier lifestyles of a time gone by. Still, the local children loved their respective communities. "During World War II, all the kids got involved," Georganna remembered. "We helped out with the paper drives and collected scrap metal for the war effort. We also had regular blackout drills. The Girl Scouts and Boy Scouts were big back then, and we did a lot of volunteering."

Much like the pioneer children of the past, Georganna and her friends spent their summers engaging in simple pleasures and games. "Our days were spent at the swimming pool in Cripple Creek, or picnicking, or going to the Lunch Car in Cripple Creek for lunch. Evenings we spent playing Kick the Can or Devil on the Doorstep. Slumber parties were very popular. In the wintertime, we went ice-skating every weekend. All the kids had skates. A special social evening in those days was attending the melodrama. We would dress up in our best and boo and hiss at the show."

Georganna also learned she suffered a similar plight to families of yesteryear while growing up. "When I was 55, I learned why we moved back and forth so much. My father gambled. One night, he bet the car and lost. He bet the house and lost. He knew his luck would change, so he bet the barbershop . . . and *lost*."

— Georganna Peiffer
Board member of the Cripple Creek District Museum
and Melissa Trenary
Archivist of the Cripple Creek District Museum

A wagon is decked out with wildflowers in Victor during the 1890s. Participants gathered as many wildflowers as possible and wove them into the spokes of the wheels and along their wagons. The occupants of the wagon in this image are dressed in their best and probably preparing to take part in a parade.

In spite of a devastating fire just three months prior, citizens of Cripple Creek turned out in force for the Fourth of July in 1896. This image was captured by photographer William Gillen, and the celebration looks to be taking place at a large canvas tent. Residents of the Cripple Creek District loved such events, which featured parades, picnics, horse races, dances, and carnival-type activities. Independence Day appears to have been the most-revered holiday celebration in the district.

Early pioneers have donned their best suits to pose for this image, taken in 1893. Five of the young men are identified, in no particular order, as Leslie Beery, Walter Warrington, Horace "Huss" Whorton, Allen Burris, and Leonard Phillips. Beery remained a resident of the district until his death in 1939.

Two men pose in front of their home at Mound City in June 1893. Note the bicycle, known in its day as the "high wheeler." Such sports equipment was expensive to come by. The presence of such an item in Mound City at such an early date indicates a true desire for pioneers to keep up with the times.

Pets were very popular in the Victorian era. Most families owned a dog or two. While most exotic pets were typically owned by the upper class, the middle and lower classes had their share of eccentric pet owners. The Jones family of Cripple Creek was the proud owner of this pampered mountain lion named Mike, who was likely captured somewhere around the district.

The Gold Coin Mine was staked in the heart of downtown Victor by Frank and Harry Woods in 1895. The brothers intended to build a hotel but discovered a gold vein instead. So wealthy were the Woods that the new mine, constructed following the fire of 1899, even had stained-glass windows. One miner was heard to comment, "It is too damn much like working in a church!"

The Gold Coin Club was very unique in that it was a place of recreation intended specifically for miners. Located across from the mine of the same name in Victor, the club included a ballroom, gymnasium, bowling alley, pool tables, dining rooms, and a 700-volume library. There was a downside: Gold Coin miners were actually required to enter the club after each shift, strip, and shower to keep them from "accidentally" taking any gold home with them.

Catholic bishop Nicholas Matz sent Rev. T. Volpe from Denver to build St. Peter's Church in Cripple Creek in 1892. Rev. William Morris set the first mass for Easter Sunday in 1898. In 1901, a Catholic school was also built. All were served by the Sisters of Mercy. Today, St. Peter's Church, St. Andrew's Episcopal Church, and the Cripple Creek Baptist Church still serve Cripple Creek.

In this extremely rare photograph, a young elephant can be seen making its way down Bennett Avenue in Cripple Creek. The elephant was part of the Lemen Bros. Circus, which was in town for its World Monster Show on May 27, 1898. The elephant, seen in front of the T.R. Lorimer building, was herded through the city as part of the show's daily Grand Free Street Parade.

This photograph was taken from the third-floor balcony of the Midland Terminal Railroad Depot in Cripple Creek around 1898. Several prominent buildings are visible down Bennett Avenue, including the Colorado Trading & Transfer Company building on the left and the National Hotel (with its tall tower) on the right. The depot opened in December 1895, was in service until 1949, and became part of the Cripple Creek District Museum in 1953.

Not all Victorians were stiff and serious. These gals seem to be having a blast together as they play on an ore cart. This image is one of a series from a c. 1898 photograph album that included the elephant on Bennett Avenue in Cripple Creek.

By the late 1890s, almost anything was obtainable in the Cripple Creek District, including purebred dogs. Here, an unidentified youngster is posed beside a great Saint Bernard. Other luxuries in the district included department stores, fancy eating houses, a number of schools, telephone service, electricity, and several daily trains that could deliver items from Colorado Springs and Canon City.

Victorian apartments were small by today's standards, yet they were quite often lavishly appointed. This photograph shows the parlor of Judge John W. Beaman at 261 East Carr Avenue. Beaman, his wife, Huldah (behind the desk), and daughter, Ella, are pictured in the image. The Beamans were in Cripple Creek for only a short time.

Dozens of stores were located throughout the Cripple Creek District. Pictured here is J.M. Watt's Mercantile at Fourth Street and Bennett Avenue in Cripple Creek around 1916. Canned food, bulk items, and fresh fruit indicate this was a grocery store. The man behind the counter is not identified. Other people in the image are, from left to right, Bob Hall, Fritz Burkhart, Jack Stevenson, Ralph Jamison, and Pauline Johnson.

The man in this image is believed to be John T. Fitzell, who moved to Cripple Creek from Denver in 1900 and managed the Cripple Creek Laundry Company. Housewives and single women also offered custom laundry services, usually at lower prices.

Like any boom camp, the cities of Cripple Creek District were not complete without a number of saloons, gambling halls, dance halls, and bordellos. Pictured here is Kilday and Weld's White House Saloon in Cripple Creek around 1893. Note the donkey that was brought in for the photograph, which was taken by photographer William Gillen.

Cripple Creek's baseball team, the Cripple Creek Districts, played against other local towns. By 1897, baseball teams could be found in Altman, Anaconda, Elkton, and Victor. Leland Evans, a cashier at the Midland Terminal Railroad Depot in Cripple Creek, actually landed a contract with the Chicago Cubs. His future was set in gold—until he fell from the platform in the rear of the depot and broke both of his arms.

Drinking was a most-favored pastime for district residents—especially young single men who had nothing better to do between mining shifts. Here, a group of boys from the Anchoria-Leland Mine stage a mock fight for the benefit of the camera. Note the numerous pin-up girls adorning the wall in the background.

Pictured above is a worker at the hoist inside a Cripple Creek mine. This magnificent piece of machinery was used to bring men, gold ore, and supplies up and down mining shafts. The "hoist man" used a series of levers and peddles to operate the mechanism. The round white dial indicated the level of the mine the hoist was at, and those above or below used a bell system to indicate the level they were on. Upon hearing the bell, the hoist man could raise or lower the hoist. Hoists were very dangerous, as most were not enclosed.

Not all residents of the Cripple Creek District were miners. At left is 24-year-old Walter George Wagner, who realized his dream to work as a cowboy while living at Cameron. This image is one of several George had taken of himself and his home. The back is inscribed, "To the folks at home . . . from the Bronco Buster, Cameron, Colo. Dec. 3 1900."

Walter George Wagner's bedroom at his home on Hoosier Avenue in Cameron was indeed fancy for the time. The lace doilies, the portiere curtain hanging in the double doorway, fancy rugs, the gas chandelier, and other adornments in the parlor show signs of wealth. Note the bobcat rug and Wagner's gun, hanging in its holster from the mirror. Other images from the Wagner home include a lavish parlor and the exterior of the home, which had a large, fenced front yard.

Contrary to the stereotypical image of Western sheriffs, officers of the Cripple Creek Police Department sported modern suits and hats and street shoes versus cowboy boots. Organized in 1892, the department has lost four officers in the line of duty: patrolman E.T. Clark in 1901, night patrolman Albert Smith in 1908, night marshal Harvey Calvin Neese in 1920, and police and fire chief Morris Dolan in 1940.

Myers Avenue is pictured here, looking west from Fourth Street around 1900. Bonton Hall, the Bijou, and the Red Light all served liquor and entertainment by the "sporting ladies" of the red-light district. Myers Avenue was home to upwards of 300 prostitutes at any given time. Houses of prostitution included anything from a brothel above one of several saloons to one-room cribs to fancy parlor houses.

Poverty Gulch, Cripple Creek's poorest neighborhood, was located at the east end of Myers Avenue just beyond the city limits. Prostitutes, gamblers, and alcoholics were known to frequent Poverty Gulch, which was typically lined with ramshackle houses and business buildings. The gulch was accessible by crossing under the Midland Terminal Railroad trestle.

Cast members from the Grand Opera House, Cripple Creek's finest theater, line up in their costumes. Ironically, "the Grand" was located in the heart of the red-light district. Even so, the theater was well attended by respectable citizens. Girls from the "row" were allowed to attend—on the condition that they use a side door and sit in the back of the theater.

In 1900, lawyer J. Maurice Finn built a 26-room mansion, the Towers, solely in anticipation of a visit from US vice president Theodore Roosevelt in early 1901. During his first visit to the Cripple Creek District in 1899, the then–New York governor was nearly mobbed by an angry crowd for his support of silver coinage versus gold. Nonetheless, Roosevelt made good on his promise to visit again in 1901. A grand gala was planned at the Towers, but due to time constraints, Roosevelt never got past the front porch. The citizens of Cripple Creek named the $50,000 structure "Finn's Folly." The home, which was poorly constructed to begin with, was dismantled in 1907.

When Roosevelt returned to the Cripple Creek District in 1901, this standard-gauge engine of the Colorado Springs & Cripple Creek District Railroad was decked out to greet him. Apologetic residents from three years prior rolled out the red carpet, and Roosevelt enjoyed his second visit much more than he had the first. At a reception line in Victor, it was said the vice president shook hands with every single resident.

In a time when death occurred suddenly and with alarming frequency, Victorians countered their losses with respectful customs regarding their dead. A popular pastime was to visit the graves of loved ones, often with a picnic lunch. Here, two children pose at the grave of Nellie Lesher, who was perhaps a sibling, at Mount Pisgah Cemetery.

Miners demonstrate using an air drill inside a mine around 1908. Air drills were both heavy and dangerous and usually required two or more men to operate them. Note the miners in this image wear no protective gear, like helmets. Such equipment seems primitive by today's standards but was very modern for its time.

Workers pose for the camera at the Mary McKinney Mine. Some of them hold special candleholders fashioned from steel. The candleholders could be carried, and the sharp end could be jammed into a crevice to provide light while working. Named for the wife of mine owner J.R. McKinney, the Mary McKinney was among the largest mines in Anaconda. It closed in 1953 after producing $11 million in gold.

The Gold Coin Mine looms over striking miners in downtown Victor in 1904 during the district's infamous labor wars of 1903–1904. The miners wanted better pay and working conditions. They were backed by the Western Federation of Miners, which fought to form a union. Numerous deaths, the deportation of more than 200 union miners, and a ban on organized labor made the strike one of the most bloody and violent in Colorado's history.

The 1903–1904 labor wars were so violent that martial law was declared. Striking miners were tried at the Teller County Courthouse, while gunmen were posted in the windows to keep peace. Here, a Gatling gun is posted in front of the Gold Mining Stock Exchange building at the corner of Fourth Street and Bennett Avenue in Cripple Creek. The gun may have been aimed at the Midland Terminal Depot, where striking miners were deported after their trials.

Miner R.A. Smith appears very unhappy about having his mug shot taken at the Teller County Jail in Cripple Creek during the labor wars of 1903–1904. Many deported miners were beaten and robbed on the trains out of town before being dropped off at the state line. In some instances, their captors fired guns over the men's heads to emphasize a warning to not return.

The Florence & Cripple Creek Railroad station in the town of Independence was nearly destroyed by a bomb during the labor dispute of 1903–1904. Thirteen nonunion miners were killed, and many more were wounded. Harry Orchard, an activist for the Western Federation of Miners, confessed to the act. His actions turned the general public's sentiment away from the striking miners and were key factors in the ultimate collapse of union labor in the Cripple Creek District.

Hearses carry the bodies of miners for burial following the explosion at Independence. In this image, the wagons make their way down Diamond Avenue in Victor. In the coming months, more miners died in skirmishes as neighbors and even families were pitted against each other. The strike lasted 15 months.

Altman Colo
View 2 – 04

Life was not easy in the Cripple Creek District. Living at high altitudes subjected pioneers to colder temperatures, unpredictable weather, and long winter months. Since mining was a year-round occupation, residents had no choice but to ride out such hazards. Snowstorms and hailstorms were known to hit during the summer months, temporarily paralyzing towns.

Sisters Hazel (left) and Mildred Owens step outside for a break from the Mountain Bell Telephone Company in 1920. Nicknamed "hello girls," the women were identified as the "chief operators" on the back of this photograph. The phone company was located on the east side of Third Street between Bennett and Carr Avenues in Cripple Creek.

Ceylon Fianna Stumpff Beard was the only daughter of Emma and Sam Stumpff. Her father built the fourth cabin in the Cripple Creek District. Born in 1895 with vision and hearing impairments, Ceylon was showered with affection by her parents and even attended a typing school. She once claimed that heavyweight Jack Dempsey taught her to box against school bullies.

Second-, third-, and fourth-grade schoolchildren gather in Anaconda on October 2, 1911. Only the students' teacher, Miss Millan, is identified—but she does not appear in the photograph. Nearly all of the towns in the Cripple Creek District had schools, many of them one-room affairs. Some, such as Cripple Creek and Victor, built several larger schools to accommodate their growing student bodies.

A bronco buster hangs on to his horse as the crowd watches in Victor, possibly during a Labor Day celebration. As one of the only modes of transportation, horses were an ever-present sight throughout all of the towns in the Cripple Creek District.

Four 1906 graduates from Cripple Creek High School dare to show their ankles as three classmates look on. Such a bold act would have been frowned upon by their mothers, but these young ladies appear to be having too much fun to worry about the trouble that might lie ahead.

Boxing was amongst the greatest American pastimes during
the Victorian era. Early newspapers indicate that Christmas
and Thanksgiving proved especially popular times to
schedule boxing matches between famous pugilists. A great
many boxers, such as the unidentified man above, aspired
to start their careers in the Cripple Creek District. Boxing
greats of the era included Jack Johnson, George Copeland,
Mexican Pete Everett, George Dixon, and Jack Dempsey.

JACK DEMPSEY

Jack Dempsey was born in Manassa, Colorado, in 1895. He
came to Cripple Creek in 1913 as a miner but soon became
involved in boxing under the name Kid Blackie. Dempsey
obtained his first knockout in a fight in Cripple Creek. He
went on to become one of the greatest boxers of the 20th
century, beating Jess Willard for the heavyweight title in 1919.

Cripple Creek's Bennett Avenue is shown following the blizzard of 1913. The storm began on December 4. Within 24 hours, drifts 10 to 20 feet deep had paralyzed the entire district. A Midland Terminal train became stranded on Victor Pass, at 10,000 feet, just outside of Goldfield. Twenty-five train passengers trekked through the drifts to safety, but it took five more days to clear the tracks. The blizzard, which also affected other towns throughout Colorado, was deemed the worst ever seen in the state.

The blizzard of 1913 left the Cripple Creek District paralyzed for nearly a week. Drifts more than 20 feet deep were recorded along local rail lines. This 11-foot rotary plow, borrowed from the Colorado Midland Railway, arrived in Cripple Creek at noon on December 11, 1913. Its journey from Victor had taken nearly 24 hours.

Pictured above is Cripple Creek High School's football team in 1914. The boys' jerseys appear to be homemade. Termed "leatherheads," early football teams sported little protective gear and helmets made only from leather. Early on, sports became an integral part of life in the Cripple Creek District.

Union Park, on the southern edge of Cripple Creek, was the center of outdoor amusement in the district for nearly 30 years. Baseball, Wild West shows, and horse races were popular summertime events. In this image, numerous cars parked on the hill above the park indicate the popularity of sports during the 1920s.

The sitting room in the Imperial Hotel is lavishly furnished in this image taken around 1915. Two of the women and children may be Ursula Long and her daughter Alice. Ursula and her husband, George, purchased the hotel in 1910. When the Mackin family bought the hotel from the Longs in 1946, they renovated the rooms and began Cripple Creek's world-famous melodrama shows. The sitting room, located next to the lobby, became the Red Rooster Bar.

The Vernon Peiffer family takes an automobile trip around 1913. Cars were a rare commodity in the Cripple Creek District at the time. It is said that the first vehicle to make the trek to Cripple Creek came up Shelf Road from Canon City. The vehicle had to make part of the journey in reverse in an effort to achieve the lowest gear while coming up a hill.

Five

TURNING GHOST

Art Tremayne was born on October 15, 1917, to Richard and Martha Tremayne. At that time, the Cripple Creek District's population was dwindling, as mining hard rock gold had become so expensive that it outweighed what the gold was worth. Hundreds of residents, some of them living in the district since the gold boom began, were seeking greener pastures. To complicate matters, World War I was looming on the horizon as a worldwide influenza epidemic plagued the district. Art and his mother both contracted the illness, but only Art survived.

Thus, Art grew up at his father's dairy outside of town. Cripple Creek was a small world that included empty houses and business buildings, but to Art, it was always home. "We had the Isis Theatre; it used to be 10¢ for a movie," he remembered. "On Friday, after school, I would clean it so I would get in free."

Art also remembered there were at least four large stores and a few neighborhood groceries scattered around town. Cripple Creek remained a close-knit community. Halloween pranks, homemade Thanksgiving dinners, and bags of candy at Christmas made for simple but fun holidays. Games included kicking a ball over a building while someone on the other side tried to catch it. When he was about 12, Art bought a used Ford Model T for just $7.50 that actually ran. No one seemed to worry about a 12-year-old driving a car, he said, and he eventually sold it for a 20-20 rifle and $25.

Of the 13 students in Art's graduating class, nine (including Art) went on to college. Some returned to live their lives in Cripple Creek. When asked if he would have chosen somewhere else to spend his life, Art shook his head, smiled, and said, "I loved growing up here. I wouldn't live anywhere else."

—Jan Collins
Director of the Cripple Creek District Museum
and Art Tremayne
Board member of the Cripple Creek District Museum

While working for the Cresson Mine in 1914, superintendent Richard Roelofs found a natural geode measuring 8,000 cubic feet. Known as the Cresson Vug, the inside of the large room was literally coated in gold flakes. Miners at the Cresson scraped more than $1.2 million in gold off the walls with their fingers in less than a week! The Cresson Vug was the last great gold discovery in the Cripple Creek District.

By 1920, the luxurious National Hotel at Bennett Avenue and Fourth Street in Cripple Creek had been torn down. Once a five-star hotel, the National was the premier place for visiting investors and businessmen to meet. Amenities at the National included a restaurant, fancy bar, limousine service from the Midland Terminal Depot, and beautiful rooms. Millionaire Winfield Scott Stratton signed a 99-year lease on a top-floor suite, paying in advance.

Victor's largest theater, the Victor Opera House, burned in 1920. Unfortunately, the insurance was barely enough to cover the great pipe organ inside. The opera house was never rebuilt, since the town was fading in population anyway. In time, almost all of the theaters in the district burned or were torn down.

Cripple Creekers rally along Bennett Avenue to support soldiers as they leave for Europe to fight in World War I. More than 250 young men from the district were enlisted in 1917 and 1918.

Above is the 1924 Cripple Creek High School girls' basketball team. Despite a shrinking student body, schoolchildren in the Cripple Creek District continued receiving a well-rounded education that included sports. Basketball and football were prominent in the curriculum.

Cripple Creek High School, amazingly enough, even had a swimming pool beginning in the 1930s. The idea probably received much support by teacher Leslie Wilkinson, who later became a principal and superintendent at the school. Longtime residents of the district still fondly remember the pool, which has since been filled in.

Dozens of lodges and clubs were present in the Cripple Creek District. They included the Elks, Eagles, Masons, Knights of Pythias, Order of the Redmen, Odd Fellows, Woodmen of the World, and others. Here, Eastern Star members celebrate Halloween with a costume ball during the 1930s.

In this photograph is a view looking west down Bennett Avenue in Cripple Creek during the 1930s. There were still as many as 135 active mines during that time, so Cripple Creek never really felt the effects of the Great Depression. Men had jobs, and food was on the table. Note Cripple Creek's only stoplight, visible in the center of the photograph at Second Street and Bennett Avenue.

Mining continued in the Cripple Creek District through the Depression. During the 1930s, the Cameron Mine opened near the townsite of Cameron on the eastern edge of the district. The mining operations were financially backed by Welch's Grape Juice Company. Hereford Peiffer was the superintendent of the mine during its short, four-year operation.

The Cripple Creek High School boys' basketball team won the district championship in 1933–1934. The boys in the photograph are identified by number: Jim Housel (no. 10), Curtis Miller (no. 3), Art Tremayne (no. 4), Kendall Hanes (no. 7), James Cayton (no. 8), Randolph Joplin (no. 13), Henry Hart (no. 12), and Herbert Nichols (no. 9).

By the 1930s, passenger traffic on the Midland Terminal Railroad had dwindled tremendously. Full passenger service was replaced with an electric streetcar that was converted to use gasoline. The Midland's Motor 101 was nicknamed "the Puddle Jumper" and quickly became a popular mode of transportation within the district. A one-way ticket between Cripple Creek and Victor only cost a nickel.

Alumni from Cripple Creek High School gather for a reunion in 1935. Those present had graduated between 1897 and 1934. During the 1940s, high schools in Cripple Creek and Victor combined into one school at Cripple Creek.

Upon graduating from high school in Cripple Creek and attending college in Colorado Springs, Art Tremayne returned to the district and went to work as a miner. Tremayne worked as a mucker (the person who shovels ore into carts for processing), machine man, and hoist man. In 1938, a promotional photographer for the Moffat Tunnel caught Tremayne on camera as he emerged from the tunnel after a day's work.

A member of the Peters family peers out the window of their cabin in Goldfield in 1938. For roughly four decades, the Cripple Creek District in general saw few improvements to homes and business buildings. Many longtime families continued living in their homes, but other structures evolved into summer homes. Still others were abandoned and left to the elements.

Following the repeal of Prohibition, the first tavern in Teller County to procure a liquor license was the Cripple Creek Inn on Bennett Avenue in Cripple Creek. The bar was opened by Bert Bergstrom in 1934. During the 1940s, the "CCI" was a favorite watering hole for local residents. This image is thought to date to World War II, judging by the gentleman in uniform.

During World War II, the Cripple Creek District joined nationwide efforts to conserve, salvage, and recycle as part of the war effort. Here, officers from the Cripple Creek Elks lodge are pictured with Boy Scouts during a War Production Board meeting. Troy Wade is pictured in the middle. Some of the other men are identified as Warren Hale, Guy Roalbaugh, and Eric Johnson.

The Cripple Creek High School marching band performs at Victor Gold Rush Days during the 1940s. The band was often invited to perform throughout the state. It also marched each year in the Apple Blossom Day Parade in Canon City and Donkey Derby Days in Cripple Creek.

John Wesley Evans was the Midland Terminal Railroad station agent in Cripple Creek from 1917 to 1941. He and his wife, Laura, along with their three sons and two grandchildren, lived on the third floor of the depot. Laura helped give the unconventional living quarters a "homey" feel by placing colored tissue paper over the transoms so they would look like stained glass.

Loretta Bielz Tremayne poses with her father, Arthur Vernon "Peggy" Bielz, in front of Zeke's Place in Victor in 1944. Established by Zeke Bennett in 1894, Zeke's remained a staple of Victor for over a century. For many years, the Yeager family ran the bar. Even today, many residents fondly remember Ohrt Yeager, who was famous for his signature chili.

For many years, the senior class at Cripple Creek High School held freshman initiations during the first week of school. Incoming freshmen were required to perform silly antics such as dressing up in costumes and carrying the seniors' books. Throughout the week, they also had to kneel down and recite a poem each time a senior walked by. Cripple Creek native Hereford "Bud" Peiffer is second from left in this image.

Former Colorado governor Ralph Carr, who served as governor from 1939 to 1943 (center, standing), and Lowell Thomas (smiling and looking at Carr) ride the last Midland Terminal train to Cripple Creek on February 6, 1949. Carr grew up in Cripple Creek. At the age of 18, Thomas became editor of the *Victor Daily Record*. Later, he became a famous war correspondent, author of 52 books, lecturer, and radio show host. He visited the district for the last time on September 4, 1981, and died 10 days later at the age of 89.

When the Midland Terminal Railroad's Engine 59 made its last run with a special charter from Colorado City to Cripple Creek in 1949, Lowell Thomas recorded the entire journey for radio station KRDO in Colorado Springs. The crew of that final train trip is pictured here. From left to right are Sam Houston, Charley Pressler, Gail Winters, Marvin McComb, and Walter Crain.

From 1949 to 1953, the Midland Terminal Railroad depot in Cripple Creek sat empty. The depot appeared almost lonely when this snapshot was taken from the back of the building in 1950. The man in the photograph is unidentified.

In addition to constructing St. Peter's Church, Father Volpe of Cripple Creek also spearheaded efforts to build St. Dimas Church at Gillett in 1907. When the town was abandoned, the church was used as a hay barn for many years. Today, only a few stone ruins remain.

In 1951, the high schools at Cripple Creek and Victor were combined in order to have enough football players to field a team. The move was quite successful, and the new combined team won the league championship later that year.

By the 1950s, a large number of houses in the Cripple Creek District were being used as summer homes. Pictured at left is one such home, owned by the McDonald family in 1958. The house was located on Spicer Street in Victor. Caroline (left) and Anne McDonald are seated out front.

When this home at 211 West Bennett Avenue in Cripple Creek was first constructed around 1898, it was among the most prestigious in town (inset). In time, the house was abandoned. During the 1970s, colorful murals were applied to the boarded-up windows, giving rise to rumors that the home had once been a brothel.

Pictured from left to right, longtime residents Lou Altman, Estel Linneman, Alvie Dunn, and Archie "Doc" Denman chat at Gus Conley's gas station in Cripple Creek at Second Street and Bennett Avenue. This photograph, taken by Myron Wood in 1966, bears the caption "The doctor, right, and a trio of cronies gather in a Cripple Creek gas station to kibitz on rumors of mine reopening." Denman worked as a physician in the district from 1917 until his death in 1984.

The Corner Stop Gas Station sat on the northwest corner of Second Street and Bennett Avenue for many years. The station was named for Cripple Creek's only stoplight, which was at that intersection from the 1920s until the 1950s. Bud and Georganna Peiffer purchased the business in the early 1980s and added a convenience and liquor store. The vintage car in this image was originally purchased in the district and remains privately owned in Cripple Creek today.

The Phenix Block at 256 East Bennett Avenue was built after the fires of 1896. Throughout the early part of the 20th century, this building was home to several saloons and billiard halls. Like so many buildings along Bennett Avenue, the structure sat vacant for many decades and was still boarded up when this photograph was taken during the 1980s. The building has since been renovated for use as a casino.

Six

THE TOURISM ERA

"Goin' up to Cripple Creek, goin' on the run, goin' up to Cripple Creek to have a little fun!" This song, penned in the early 1890s, says it all.

Cripple Creek has always held an allure for visitors. Why do people go? What's shakin'?

Shakin'? By 1900, ladies wearing the finest Paris fashions were shakin' their bustles. The green leaves of spring and the quaking gold aspen in the fall were shakin.' The shakin' could possibly have been the dice in Johnny Nolon's Saloon at the end of the 20th century and again at the beginning of the 21st with legalized gambling. The shakin' could be the dancers at the Grand or Lyric Opera Houses, the Gold Bar Room's melodrama show at the Imperial Hotel, or the Butte Theater.

What about the railroads that carried gold down the mountain and supplies back up? Tourists could ride the train and see the beautiful scenery or pick wildflowers along the way. Today, the old railroads are scenic byways. Visitors can feel the rumble of the past in the Cripple Creek District Museum, the Old Homestead and the Narrow Gauge Railroad in Cripple Creek and at the Victor/Lowell Thomas Museum in Victor. Maybe the shakin' is the shiver one feels while looking at the spectacular view from the Cripple Creek Heritage Center.

The shakin' could be the elevator going 1,000 feet down at the Mollie Kathleen Mine where mining commenced a century ago. Or could it be the Cripple Creek–Victor mine tour of today?

There is another song, "Cripple Creek Desperado," about a man who came to find his little piece of gold and have a good time. Fourth of July celebrations, Gold Camp Christmases, summer wildflowers, Donkey Derby Days and Gold Rush Days—these are all still local attractions. Times have changed a little. The Desperado can't shoot out the lights anymore, but he can stroll down the streets where history was and still is being made in a unique corner of the world.

—Steve Mackin
President of the board of the Cripple Creek District Museum

The Cripple Creek Inn remained the town's most popular restaurant and tavern for more than 60 years. Advertisements in the local telephone directories boasted that the CCI was the largest saloon in the Cripple Creek District. Owner Bert Bergstrom's wife, Martha, and bartender Hereford Peiffer posed for this photograph in 1949.

Founded in 1931 to promote tourism, Donkey Derby Days has remained Cripple Creek's most popular celebration for almost 80 years. The parade was a stellar attraction at Donkey Derby Days by the 1940s. Residents and business owners made their own entries, from classic cars to homemade floats. Promoters of the event actually loaded donkeys into a trailer and traversed the state to advertise the event.

Wayne Mackin is pictured standing in front of the Imperial Hotel in Cripple Creek shortly after he and his wife, Dorothy, purchased it in May 1946. As the cracked windows show, the neglected hotel required much work to be restored to its earlier grandeur.

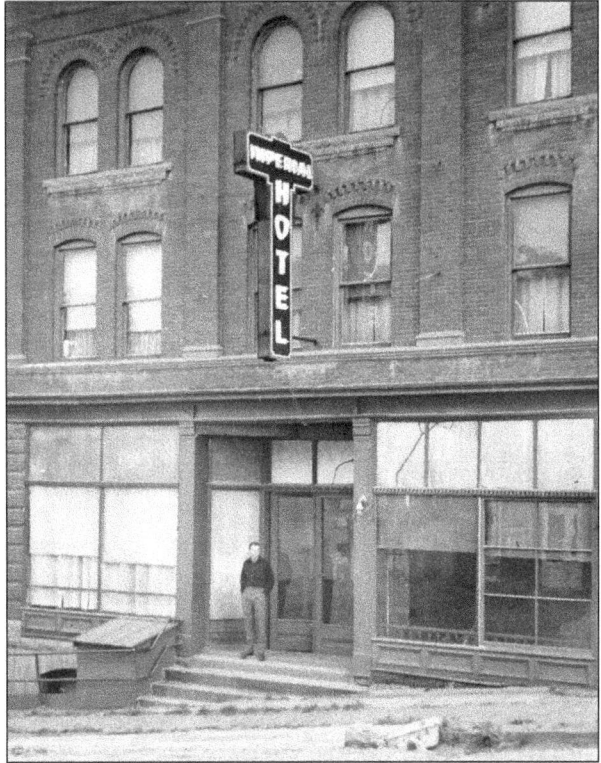

In 1947, Wayne and Dorothy Mackin began hosting Prospector Breakfasts at the Imperial Hotel. Guests were treated to breakfast and then taken to the Los Angeles Mine outside of Victor to look for gold in the old mine dumps.

Lowell Thomas (left), Mabel Barbee Lee, and Merrill Shoup are seen here at the Golden Cycle Mill. Shoup, whose family once purchased the Midland Terminal Railroad to save it from closing, also owned the mill. During their visit Thomas, Lee, and Shoup watched miners pour 99.9-percent pure gold into solid bricks. The brick bars the men are holding in this image weighed about 1,300 troy ounces, worth $1.69 million at today's prices.

Max Morath sits at his famous piano in the Imperial Hotel's Gold Bar Room Theatre some time in the 1950s, and again at the Red Rooster Bar (inset) around 2000. Still known as "the Ragtime Man," Morath was among those responsible for spearheading the national ragtime piano revival during the 1970s. Even today, the Red Rooster Bar sports 210 pieces of rooster art that include sculptures, ceramics, and paintings.

The melodrama shows at the Imperial attracted thousands of people each season. In this image, audience members sport black paper moustaches given out at the show in 1964. Pictured are, from left to right, (first row) Ruth Shoup, Richard "Dick" Johnson, Wilhemina Denman, Hazel Bunker, Troy Wade, and Peg Giddings; (second row) Jack Shoup, Miriam Shoup, Dr. Archie "Cam" Denman, and Zell Wade.

Millionaire heir Blevins Davis purchased the former Midland Terminal Railroad Depot in Cripple Creek and instructed his friend Richard Johnson to open the Cripple Creek District Museum. A grand opening was held on June 14, 1953, and Gov. Dan Thornton was an honored guest. Seen from left to right are (first row) Richard "Dick" Johnson, Ralph Giddings, Troy Wade, and Governor Thornton; (second row) Miriam Shoup, Dorothy Mackin, Wilhemina Denman, Norma Hill, First Lady Jessie Thornton, and Margaret Giddings.

Built by Pearl DeVere following the fire of 1896, the Old Homestead operated as Cripple Creek's most famous and elegant house of ill repute until about 1919. Fred and Pat Mentzer purchased the house in 1950 and opened it as a museum in 1958. Lodi and Harold Hern purchased the museum during the 1960s, and Lodi is still considered the madam of the Old Homestead today.

The Spoilers, based on the novel by Rex Beach, was first produced at the Imperial in 1959. The first man on the left is singer-songwriter Johnny Horton. Third from left is Tom Paxton, who became a prolific songwriter. Fourth from the left is Phil Webber, who ended up establishing one of the most successful rehabilitation facilities in the United States. Famous visitors to the melodrama shows include former governor Ralph Carr, Lowell Thomas, Walt Disney, Mary Tyler Moore, and Lily Ponds.

Astrologist Linda Goodman wrote such famous books as *Sun Signs* and *Love Signs* while living in Cripple Creek between the 1960s and 1980s. Her last book, *Gooberz* (1989), contains references to many longtime area residents. Many locals still remember enjoying movies, food, and drinks with her. Goodman passed away in 1995.

Mabel Barbee Lee, left, moved to Cripple Creek as a young girl and later wrote about her life in Cripple Creek's early days. Even today, her best-known book, *Cripple Creek Days*, remains a good example of life in the gold camp and covers many events of the time. In this image, Lee is seen in Cripple Creek with Lowell Thomas (center) and Rufus "the Hardrock Poet" Porter during a 1967 reunion.

The donkeys of the Cripple Creek District remain a popular attraction. Here, former Cripple Creek mayor Henry "June" Hack is seen feeding the herd in front of his Cripple Creek grocery store during the 1960s. Today, the Two Mile High Club looks after a herd of donkeys, and the Cripple Creek District Museum Gift Shop sells healthy snacks for visitors to feed them.

During the 1970s and 1980s, one of the most popular children's competitions during Donkey Derby Days was the greased pig race. A small pig would be greased down, and the children had to attempt to catch it. Whoever could catch the pig and hang onto it for a set amount of time was the winner.

Seven

TODAY'S CRIPPLE CREEK DISTRICT

The Cripple Creek District of today is an amazing melting pot of roughly 2,000 citizens. Some are descendants from the homesteaders and gold-seekers who came here more than a century ago. Others have lived here 5, 10, or 30 years after falling in love with the district's history, unsurpassed mountain views, and unique way of life. All agree there is no other place on earth quite like this.

Only three of the 20 towns in the district remain. Cripple Creek is home to the district's only school, bank, and gas station, as well as casinos, museums, shops, restaurants, and other attractions that bring visitors to town year round. Victor remains a workingman's town with a number of shops and restaurants, the Victor/Lowell Thomas Museum, and the beautiful Victor Hotel. Goldfield survives as a bedroom community to Victor with several residents. Donkey Derby Days, Gold Rush Days, and other annual events draw people to the district throughout the year.

Gold is still mined here too, represented by a few privately owned mines, including a most unique turquoise mine. The massive Cripple Creek–Victor Mine also operates in the hills around the towns, employing roughly 300 miners who carry on the traditions of a century ago.

Most of the district's residents live here all year long. Together, they work and live, weather the hard winters, and enjoy the warm summers. They gather at community celebrations, enjoy the outdoors, and marvel at how lucky they are to live in such a beautiful place. And, of course, they enjoy the fabulous story the district has to offer about its historic beginnings and survival as a tourist mecca. The charm of the Cripple Creek District is indeed its history, which continues to be preserved for future generations to enjoy.

—Corey Collins
Restorationist at the Cripple Creek District Museum

The Mollie Kathleen Mine is one of the oldest producing mines in the district. Mollie Kathleen Gortner defied local businessmen in 1893 when she insisted on staking the mine herself instead of waiting for her husband to do it for her. The mine began offering public tours in the 1940s and remains a popular attraction today.

The completion of the Carlton Drainage Tunnel in 1941 and construction of the Carlton Mill outside of Victor in 1951 brought about a slight increase in gold production. Pictured here in 1961 is a gold pour at the mill. Heavy gloves were necessary as the hot, molten gold was poured. The closing of the mill in 1961 signified the official end to the Cripple Creek District's first mining era. The mill was torn down in 1996.

The Cripple Creek & Victor Narrow Gauge Railroad is one of Cripple Creek's most popular summertime attractions. The railroad, located next to the Cripple Creek District Museum, made its first run on June 28, 1967. The 45-minute trip runs from Cripple Creek to the site of Anaconda and back.

During the 1980s, a large group of local young people nicknamed themselves the Gonzos. The group became famous for their escapades around the Cripple Creek District. Most popular were the wild and crazy floats they built every year for the Donkey Derby Days parade. Year after year, the Gonzos won first place for their creations.

The onset of legalized gaming in 1991 did much to change the face of Cripple Creek's downtown area. Shops closed, and signs—such as that of the Sarsaparilla Saloon at Third Street and Bennett Avenue, shown at left—were replaced by casino marquees. A number of structures were altered, updated, built onto, or torn down as Cripple Creek received its first face-lift in more than a century.

Gambling has dramatically improved Cripple Creek's monetary status, as well as that of other towns around the state. Portions of Colorado's gaming proceeds go toward statewide historic preservation efforts. Above are "then and now" images of the historic Bell Brothers building on Bennett Avenue in Cripple Creek, which was restored in the 1990s. Today, the structure is home to the Cripple Creek Police Department.

In Cripple Creek, historic preservation funds have allowed for the restoration of dozens of buildings. In 1996, the former Butte Opera House on Bennett Avenue was renovated, and today, it hosts shows put on by the Thin Air Theatre Company. The downstairs portion houses Cripple Creek's fire department.

In 1996, the Cripple Creek District Museum received funding through the City of Cripple Creek and the Colorado State Historic Fund to restore the Colorado Trading & Transfer Company building. A new cement foundation, including a fireproof vault, was installed underneath, and the structure received needed repairs and renovations inside.

Donkey Derby Days remains one of Cripple Creek's largest events. When this photograph was taken in 1999, upwards of 1,000 people had turned out for the annual parade. Staged gunfights, dances, beer tents, craft and food vendors, children's activities, and a host of other events make Donkey Derby Days a favorite family attraction. The year 2011 marks the event's 80th anniversary.

Begun in 1895 as a "World Celebration," Victor's Gold Rush Days has evolved into a fun family affair. Live music, a parade, and mining games have remained a staple of the festivities. Here, competitors take part in a mucking contest during the 1980s. Today, the Victor/Lowell Thomas Museum preserves Victor's amazing mining history.

Beginning in 1993, the city of Cripple Creek began working with promoters to bring an annual motorcycle ride to town in recognition of military POWs and MIAs. Now termed the Salute to American Veterans, but better known as "Biker Weekend," this annual event is by far the largest in Cripple Creek. Thousands of motorcycles and enthusiasts, pictured here in 1999, come to town for a four-day celebration each August.

Museum founder Richard "Dick" Johnson (left) visits with childhood friend Dr. Scott Severens in 2002. After founding the Cripple Creek District Museum in 1953, Johnson remained on the Cripple Creek District Museum's board of directors through the rest of his life. Johnson died in 2004.

In 2006, museum board member Jeff Miller successfully saved two historic cabins from the wrecking ball. The cabin on the left was the former home of Blanche LeCroix at the ghost town of Midway. On the right is a typical miner's cabin from Cripple Creek. In 2009, the City of Cripple Creek donated both structures to the Cripple Creek District Museum.

The Colorado Trading & Transfer Company building is the only remaining wooden commercial structure in Cripple Creek. Today, the building houses the museum gift shop, displays, an office, an art gallery, and adequate storage space in the basement.

126

The Cripple Creek District Museum was founded in 1953 to preserve, protect, interpret, and share the history of the entire Cripple Creek District and Teller County. Over time, the museum has acquired literally millions of artifacts including documents, photographs, books, maps, newspapers, furnishings, clothing, personal items, mineral specimens, mining equipment, and other memorabilia directly related to the history of the district. The museum is proud to be the largest and oldest historical institution in the Pike's Peak region. In 2010, *True West* magazine named the museum a Top 10 Western Museum. A small paid staff and volunteers work within the archives and assist patrons with genealogical and historical research. As a nonprofit corporation, the museum operates solely on the sale of tickets, photographs, and gifts, donations, and grants. Even today, descendants of pioneers, former residents, and history buffs continue to donate items to the museum regularly. The 1895 Midland Terminal Railroad Depot, the 1894 Colorado Trading & Transfer Company building, two cabins, an assay office, and a headframe from the Pinnacle Mine at the ghost town of Cameron make for a most worthwhile visit. The museum is open year round and can be contacted by visiting the website at www.cripple-creek.org.

Visit us at
arcadiapublishing.com

www.ingramcontent.com/pod-product-compliance
Lightning Source LLC
Chambersburg PA
CBHW080616110426
42813CB00006B/1527